First published 1999 AD
This edition © Wooden Books Ltd 2002 AD
Illustrations pgs 26, 32, 34, 36, 43b
& 48 © J. R. Kirkham 2001

Published by Wooden Books Ltd.
8A Market Place, Glastonbury, Somerset

British Library Cataloguing in Publication Data
Johnson, P. A.
Runic Inscriptions in Great Britain

A CIP catalogue record for this important book
is available from the British Library

ISBN 1 904263 40 2

Printed and bound in Shanghai, China
by Shanghai iPrinting Co., Ltd.
100% recycled papers.

WOODEN
BOOKS

RUNIC INSCRIPTIONS
IN GREAT BRITAIN

by
Paul Johnson

with additional illustrations by John Kirkham

Most of the illustrations have been reproduced from George Stephens'
four volumes: "The Old-Northern Runic Monuments of Scandinavia and
England" (1866-1901), with lithographs by J. Magnus Petersen. The
illustrations on pages 26, 32, 34, 36, 43(b) and 48 were meticulously
drawn by John Kirkham.

Further reading, academic first & esoteric last: "An Introduction to English
Runes" by R. I. Page, "Runes" by R. V. W. Elliot, "Rudiments of Runelore"
by S. Pollington and "Leaves of Yggdrasil" by F. Aswynn.

Many thanks to the following for their help and support:
Benson, Prof. M Barnes and the The Viking Society for Northern Research
at the UCL, Andrew Tester and the Suffolk County Archaeological Services,
Dr. Helen Geake and the Archaeology Department at the Castle Museum in
Norwich, Stephen Grundy, John Kirkham and Steve Pollington.

CONTENTS

*The Sandwich Stone, probably the only surviving Heathen runic stone of
Anglo-Saxon England. One of a pair in the Royal Museum, Canterbury*

INTRODUCTION

The ancient magical letters of the runic alphabets have appeared in inscriptions from the first century until late Medieval times and have been found scattered right across continental Europe and beyond. They have been used for a multitude of different purposes during their rich history.

They were first etched and inscribed upon a vast diversity of artifacts and objects, both for practical and for magical purposes. They were used as an oracular device and as magical symbols, as calendars, in cryptology and in riddles and poems. Runes were also used as personal, tradesman and stonemason's marks, to convey straightforward messages and as just plain old graffiti.

So, as much of the past is claimed by earth and water, the soils and rivers of this green isle still continue to turn up old artifacts and objects bearing runes and this small book serves, I hope, as an introduction to some of the more interesting examples.

Herne Hill, London

1

ORIGINS

when is an ark an orc?

The most intriguing of characters, runes, were born out of the mists of Old Europe and their beginnings, almost like the several meanings and derivatives of the word itself, remain secretive and mysterious.

It seems likely that the first runic alphabet was founded upon the early Mediterranean alphabets such as the North Italic script and the Etruscan and Roman alphabets. However, many of these magical runic symbols predate this amalgamation and can be seen in the numerous ancient pictographs and ideograms which are found scattered across Europe. Perhaps, at some point, sound, symbol and concept fused, subsequently forming the runic alphabet.

Runes developed as a practical alphabet and also as a magical script from around the second century onward. The first working alphabet of 24 runes is known as the Elder Fuþark (pronounced "foothark") and is named after the first six characters of the runic alphabet. Traditionally the Fuþark was split into three 'Ættir', Old Icelandic for family or group of eight.

As language evolved across old Europe new runic alphabets were developed to accommodate these linguistic changes.

The Common Germanic Fuþark

ᚠ ᚢ ᚦ ᚨ ᚱ ᚲ ᚷ ᚹ
f *u* *þ* *a* *r* *k* *g* *w*

ᚺ ᚾ ᛁ ᛃ ᛈ ᛉ ᛋ
h *n* *i* *ė* *p* *z* *s*

ᛏ ᛒ ᛖ ᛗ ᛚ ᛜ ᛟ ᛞ
t *b* *e* *m* *l* *ŋ* *o* *d*

The Anglo-Saxon Fuþorc

ᚠ ᚢ ᚦ ᛇ ᚱ ᚳ ᚷ ᚹ
f *u* *þ* *o* *r* *c* *g* *w*

ᚺ ᚾ ᛁ ᛄ ᛚ ᛈ ᛉ ᛋ
h *n* *i* *j* *eo* *p* *x* *s*

ᛏ ᛒ ᛖ ᛗ ᛚ ᚷ ᛟ ᛞ
t *b* *e* *m* *l* *ŋ* *œ* *d*

ᚪ ᚫ ᚣ ᛡ ᛠ
a *æ* *y* *ia* *eâ*

The Danish Fuþark

ᚠ ᚢ ᚦ ᚭ ᚱ ᚴ ᚼ ᚾ
f *u* *þ* *a* *r* *k* *h* *n*

ᛁ ᛅ ᛦ ᛧ ᛏ ᛒ ᛘ ᛚ
i *a* *r* *s* *t* *b* *m* *l*

The Manx-Jeran Rune Row

ᚠ ᚢ ᚦ ᚦ ᚱ ᚴ ᚼ ᚾ
f *u* *þ* *a* *r* *k* *h* *n*

ᛁ ᛆ ᛁ ᛐ ᛏ ᛓ ᛘ ᛚ ᛁ
i *a* *s* *t* *b* *m* *l* *R*

The Orkney Rune Row

ᚠ ᚢ ᚦ ᚮ ᚱ ᚴ ᚼ ᚾ
f *u* *þ* *o* *r* *k* *h* *n*

ᛁ ᛆ ᛁ ᛐ ᛒ ᛘ ᛚ ᛦ
i *a* *s* *t* *b* *m* *l* *y*

ᛐ ᛣ ᛣ ᛂ ᛁ ᚤ ᚦ
æ *ǫ* *ø* *e* *g* -

THE ANGLO-SAXON RUNE POEM

a clue from the dark ages

The runes first came to these shores in or around the fifth century with the Anglo-Saxons, who by the time of their arrival had begun to modify the elder Fuþark into the Anglo-Saxon Fuþorc. This runic alphabet continued to flourish, reaching 28 characters and, like many pagan things, was adopted and also used by the Church as a straightforward script.

Between the eighth and tenth centuries scribes recorded the Anglo-Saxon rune poem, which seems to be a condensation of rune lore in poetical formula. The original manuscript which contained the rune poem was destroyed in a great fire in 1731, but a fortunate copy was preserved in George Hickes' *Thesauraus* of 1703.

For each rune, the Latin equivalent is followed by its runic character, name and a verse describing the imagery and energy behind each rune. The poetical allusions of the Old English text are predominantly heathen although some of the poem may have been altered by the scribes to suit Christian taste.

The rune poem was primarily used as a mnemonic and contemplative device to help remember the rune name and meaning and thus the sound value.

byþ frofur. fira gehƿylcum. sceal ðeah manna gehƿylc. miclun hyt dælan.
gif he ƿile. for drihtne domes hleotan :.

byþ anmod. 7 ofer hyrned. fela frecne. beoþ feohteþ. mid hornum. mæ-
re mor stapa. þ is modig puht :.

byþ ðearle scearp. ðegna gehƿylcum. anfen-gys yfyl. ungemetun reþe.
manna gehƿylcun. ðe him mid resteþ :.

byþ ordfruma. ælcre spræce. pisdomes praþu. and pitena frofur. and
eorla gehþam. eadnyf and to hiht :.

byþ onrecyde. rinca gehƿylcum. sefte and sƿiþhƿæt. ðam ðe ritteþ on-
ufan. meare mægen heardum. ofer mil paþar :.

byþ cpicera gehþam cuþ on fyre blac and beorhtlic byrneþ oftust ðær
hi æþelingaf inne restaþ :.

gumena byþ gleng and herenyr. praþu 7 pyrþscype 7 præcna gehþam ar.
and ætpirt ðe byþ oþra leas :.

ne bruceþ ðe can peana lyt rarer and rorge and him rylfa hæþ blæb
7 blyrre and eac bynga geniht :.

byþ hpiturt corna. hpyrþt hit of heofoner lyfte. pealcaþ hit þinþer rcu-
na. peorþeþ hit to pætepe ryðþan :.

byþ nearu on breortan peorþeþ hi ðeah oft niþa bearnum to helpe and to
hæle ge hpæþpe gif hi hir hlyrtaþ æror :.

byþ ofep cealdunge metum rlidop glirnaþ glærnaþ glær hluttup gimmum geli-
curt. flop forrte ge popuht fæger anryne :.

byþ gumena hiht ðon god læteþ halig heofoner cyning hrurap ryllan
beorhte bleda beornum and ðeapfum :.

byþ utan unrmeþe tpeop. heapð hpupan fæft hypðe fyrer. pyrtrumun
underpeþyð pynan on eþle :.

byþ rymble plega. and hlehter plancum ðap pigan rittaþ on beop rele
bliþe æt romne :.

reccanð hæfþ oftuft on fenne. pexeð on patupe. punðaþ grimme. blode
bpeneð beopna gehƿylcne ðe him ænigne onfeng gedeð :.

re mannum rymble biþ on hihte ðonn hi hine fepiaþ ofer firces beþ oþ
hibhum hengert bpingeþ to lanðe :.

biþ tacna rum healbeð tpypa pel. þiþ æþelingap a biþ onfæpylðe. ofep nihta
genipu. næfpe rpiceþ :.

byþ bleda leaf. bepeþ efne rpa ðeah tanar butan tudder. biþ on telgum pli-
tig. þeah on helme hpyrted fægepe. geloben leafum lyfte getenge :.

byþ for eoplum æþelinga þyn. horf hofum planc. ðæp him hæleþ ymb. pe-
lege on picgum pprxlaþ rpnæce. 7 biþ unrtyllum æfne fnofup :.

byþ on myngþe hir magan leof. rceal þeah anpa gehƿylc oðrum rpican.
forþ ðam þpyhten pyle dome rine þ eapme flærc eopþan betæcan :.

byþ leobum langrum geþuht gif hi rculun neþan on nacan tealtum. 7 hi
ræ yþa rpyþe bpegaþ. and re bpim hengert bpiðlep ne gym :.

þær ærert mid earte denum. ge repen recgun. oþ he riðban ert. ofen þæg
gepat þæn æften pan. ður heapðingar ðone hæle nembun :.

byþ ofep leof. æghpylcum men. gif he mot ðæp. pihtep and gepyrena
on bpucan on blode bleabum oftart :.

byþ bpihtnep fond. beope mannum. mæpe metoðer leoht. mýpgþ and
to hiht eaðgum and eapmum. eallum bpice :.

byþ on eopþan. elda beapnum. flærcer fodop fepeþ gelome ofen ganoter
bæþ gapreccg fandaþ. hpæþen ac hæbbe æþele tpeope :.

biþ ofep heah. eldum byne. rtiþ on rtaþule. rtede pihte hylt. ðeah him
reohtan on firar monige :.

byþ æþelinga 7 eopla gehƿær. pyn and pyrþmynð. byþ on picge fægen. fæft-
lic on fæpelbe. fyrð geacepa rum :.

byþ ea fixa. and ðeah abpuceþ. fodrer onfalðan. hafaþ fægepne eaprd.
pætpe bepoppen. ðæp he pynnum leofaþ :.

byþ egle eopla gehƿylcun. ðonn fæftlice flærc onginneþ. hpapcolian hpupan
ceopan blac to gebebban bleða geþreopaþ. pynna gepitaþ þepa gerpicaþ :.

Hos Characteres ᚠᚢᛗᛈᛚᚳᛉᛒᛟᚷ ad alia festinans
studioso lectori interpretanda relinquo.

5

THE RUNE POEM

a new interpretation

Not much is known about the early rune-masters who created these runic alphabets and poems except that they were an elite few and belonged to an oral tradition. This modern interpretation of the rune poem presents us with a preserved insight into the Anglo-Saxon mind.

ᚠ   *Wealth is a comfort to everyone, yet each must bestow it freely, if he wants to win a good name before his Lord.*

ᚢ   *Aurochs is fierce and high horned, a savage beast, it fights with its horns, a great roamer of the moorlands it is a creature of mettle.*

ᚦ   *Thorn is extremely sharp, touching it is painful to any warrior, excessively severe for anyone who lies among them.*

ᚩ   *God is the source of all language, a pillar of wisdom and the comfort of the wise, a blessing and joy to every man.*

ᚱ   *Rad is pleasant to every warrior in the hall but strenuous for him who sits upon the back of a strong horse traversing the mile paths.*

ᚻ   Torch is known to all living creatures by its pale, bright flame;
it usually burns when nobles rest indoors.

ᚷ   Giving is the grace and honour for men, a support and glory, and
for any exile a help and sustenance when he has no other.

ᚹ   Joy is needed not by him who knows little want, pain and sorrow,
and has for himself wealth and bliss and the comfort of towns.

ᚻ   Hail is the whitest of corn, from the heights of heaven it whirls
in the wind, soon it returns to water.

ᚾ   Need constricts the heart, yet it is often a help and salvation to
the sons of men if they attend it in time.

ᛁ   Ice is very cold and extremely slippery, a floor fair to the sight,
wrought by frost, glitters like gems, clear as glass.

ᛄ   Harvest is the hope of men when Frigg heavens Queen, the
earth to give up bright fruits for rich and poor.

ᛇ   Yew is a tree with rough bark, hard and fast in the earth, the
guardian of fire, supported by roots, a joy on the homeland.

ᛈ   Peorth is always play and laughter to the proud ones, where
wives sit in the birthall blithely together.

ᛦ   *Elk-sedge most often dwells on the fen, growing in water, severely wounding and marks with blood any man who tries to take it.*

ᛋ   *Sun to seamen is always a joy, when they cross the fish's bath till the brine steed bears them to land.*

ᛏ   *Tir is a guiding mark, he keeps trust with all men, he is always on his path above the night's clouds and never fails.*

ᛒ   *Birch has no fruit yet bears shoots without seeds, glorious in its branches and laden with leaves, touching the sky.*

ᛗ   *The horse-hoof proud, is a prince's delight in the presence of warriors, when rich men on horseback mix words, and is ever a source of comfort to the restless.*

ᛗ   *Man in his merriment is dear to his kinsmen, yet each is bound to fail his fellow because Sculd by her decree wishes to commit the wretched flesh to the earth.*

ᛚ   *Water seems interminable to men if they have to venture on the rolling ship and the sea waves scare them, and the brine stallion heeds not its bridle.*

ᛝ   *Ing was first seen among the East Danes, then he went east across the waves with his wagon behind him. This is what the warriors called him.*

ᛟ The ancestral home is dear to all men, if he can enjoy there in his house whatever is right and proper in continual prosperity.

ᛗ Day, beloved of men, is heaven's messenger, the Creator's glorious light. It is a joy and comfort to rich and poor and of service to all.

ᚪ Oak feeds the pig for meat for the sons of men, it often fares over the gannet's bath. The ocean tests whether the oak keeps honourable faith.

ᚫ The Ash, precious to men, is very tall. Firm in the ground, it keeps its place securely though many men attack it.

ᛄ The Axe-hammer is a fine piece of war-gear. It is a joy and honour to every prince and warrior, fine on a horse and dependable on a journey.

ᛡ Iar is a river-fish and yet it always eats its food on land. It has a fair abode surrounded by water where it lives in happiness.

ᛦ The Grave is hateful to every man, when the flesh grows cold and the pallid body chooses the earth as its consort. Prosperity fades, joys pass away and covenants end.

THE RUNIC FUÞORC

getting to know the runes

Many of our everyday words are related by their history or etymology to Old English rune words. In this way echoes of the runes are spread throughout many of the modern North European languages.

The modern word "Fee" derives from the first rune *Feoh,* denoting cattle, or wealth, its shape also resembling bovine horns. In former times the amount of cattle an individual possessed was a measure for their wealth.

The Scottish dialectal word *Ken*, meaning 'to know' is also the esoteric illumination behind the rune *Ken*, shaped like an old firebrand. Many of the rune characters developed in this way from shapes or forms found in the surrounding natural world. *Gyfu*, denoting partnerships, resembles the crosses long made at the end of love letters. The shape of the rune *Nyd,* signifying need, may be the origin for the popular custom of 'fingers crossed'.

Observing runeshapes from these realms was once considered to be meaningful.

The Anglo-Saxon Fuþorc was used in inscriptions until around the ninth century, by which time it had again been further developed in the kingdom of Northumbria. The ninth century also saw the introduction into the British Isles of the sixteen-character Younger Fuþark brought by settling Vikings and inscribed here until the twelfth century.

The rune words of the Anglo-Saxon Fuþorc have many cognates in Old English and these words may represent related concepts and meanings of the runes.

During the foundation of Christianity upon old England's pagan soils the Latin alphabet became reintroduced and the runes coexisted alongside it through the time of the Dual Faith and right into the conversion period. Eventually the Church replaced this heathen alphabet with the characters with which I now write.

The first two familes, or *Ættir*, are shown on the next page; the rest are shown facing them.

Rune Shape	Name	Sound	Letter	Literal Meaning (OE)	Word Streams and Patterns
ᚠ	*Feoh*	f	f	cattle, wealth	OE *feorh*, life, spirit ME *fee*, payment
ᚢ	*Ur*	u	u	*aurochs*	ON *urdr*, OE *wyrd*, fate, destiny
ᚦ	*Thorn*	th	þ	*thorn*	OE *thorpe*, village
ᚩ	*Os*	o	o	mouth, speech	Latin *os*, mouth ON *ass*, God
ᚱ	*Rad*	r	r	*riding, road*	OE *rædels, riddles rædan*, to *read*, advise
ᚳ	*Cen*	c	c	firebrand, torch	Sc *ken*, to know OE *cennan*, to reveal
ᚷ	*Gyfū*	g	g	*gift*	OE *giefan*, to *give* ME *gift*
ᚹ	*Wynn*	w	w	joy	OE *wynsum, winsome* ME *wish*
ᚺ	*Hægl*	h	h	*hail*	---
ᚾ	*Nyd*	n	n	*need, necessity*	OE *nyt*, urge, duty *neod*, desire, crave
ᛁ	*Is*	i	i	*ice*	OE *isen, iron*
ᛄ	*Ger*	j	j	*year harvest*	OE *geard, garden, gearn,* ripe, ready, ME *hour*
ᛇ	*Eoh*	e	e	*yew*	OE *iw*, bright, red *ierre, yrre*, wild, excite
ᛈ	*Peorþ*	p	p	---	---
ᛉ	*Eolhx*	x	x	*elk-sedge*	---
ᛋ	*Sigel*	s	s	sun, jewel	OE *sige*, victory fallen, sunset

Rune Shape	Name	Sound	Letter	Literal Meaning (OE)	Word Streams and Patterns
↑	*Tir*	t	t	the god Tir	OE *tir*, fame honour
ᛒ	*Beorc*	b	b	*birch* tree	OE *beorgan*, protect, hide *beorh*, hill, *barrow*
ᛖ	*Eh*	e	e	horse	OE *ewa*, marriage contract
ᛗ	*Man*	m	m	*man*, human being	OE *manncynn*, *mankind*
ᛚ	*Lagu*	l	l	water	ME *lake*, *lagoon* Sc *loch*
ᛝ	*Ing*	ng	ŋ	the god Ing	OE *ing*, meadow Sc *ingle*, fire
ᛟ	*Eþel*	o	œ	homeland	OE *eþele*, noble
ᛞ	*Dæg*	d	d	*day*	OE *dægian*, *dawn* OE *dæglan*, secret
ᚪ	*Ac*	a	a	*oak*	OE *æcern*, acorn
ᚫ	*Aesc*	ae	æ	*ash*	--
ᛡ	*Yr*	y	y	--	OE *æxe yr(e)*, *axe*-hammer
ᛇ	*Ior*	io	io	river-fish, beaver, otter	--
ᛠ	*Ear*	ea	ea	grave	OE *ear*, earth, ocean, *eard*, homeland

OE - Old English, MO - Modern English,
ON - Old Norse, Sc - Scottish.

THE RUTHWELL CROSS
pagan poems, evolving rune schools

The Ruthwell Cross towers over seventeen feet high and is contained within the Ruthwell Church in Dumfries and Galloway, close to its original site. This runestone is perhaps the most impressive and elaborate piece of eighth century Northumbrian art and craftsmanship in the country.

It displays the longest recorded rune passage in the British Isles, with several additional new rune forms appearing, lengthening the existing Fuþorc into the 'Northumbrian Rune Row' of about thirty-three characters. Although now worn and incomplete the passage details a variant Northumbrian dialect and theme of the early English Poem *The Dream Of The Rood*. The poem is recorded later in the Vercelli Codex in Italy in which the Cross itself speaks of the trials of Christ.

This earlier version, with its strongly heathen overtones, may have utilised existing beliefs to enrich the newer story of the Crucifixion during the Anglo-Saxon conversion.

Parallel Heathen myths such as the similar sacrifice of Woden upon the world tree or the resurrection of Balder are themes the poem may have touched upon.

15

THE BEWCASTLE CROSS
at the centre of the world

Steep upon the wild borderlands of Scotland, quite close to Hadrian's Wall, lies the small hamlet of Bewcastle. Situated in its original position within the church grounds this runic cross is over fourteen feet high and is dated to the early eighth century, like the Ruthwell Cross a product of the dual-faith period.

Once connected to a lost cross-head the surviving shaft is intricately carved from a single block of stone and depicts traditional Christian imagery along with what may be the secular donor of the monument attired for falconry.

Earlier translations of the nine lines of runes dedicate the monument to Alcfirth, a son of King Oswiu, but now much of it is illegible. Alcfirth's father Oswiu united and ruled the early kingdoms of Deria with Bernicia which together formed Northumbria.

On the opposite side of the monument elaborate carvings depict a tree bursting with animals and plants which has been paralleled with Yggdrasil, the world-tree of heathen cosmology.

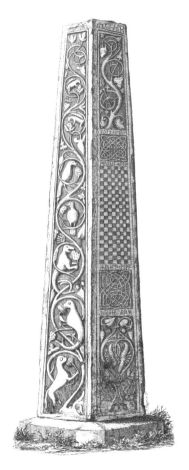

THE FALSTONE STONE
pray for his soul

Kept in the possession of the Museum of Antiquities in Newcastle-upon-Tyne this oddly shaped memorial stone was found three feet below the ground at Hawkhope hill near the village of Falstone in old Northumberland.

On the face of the stone are two inscriptions, one in Roman characters and the other in Anglo-Saxon runes reflecting the biliteracy of the time and the magical connection between the runes and the afterlife. Both sections record the same Old English memorial passage, "Eo set up a monument after Hroethberht his uncle - pray for his soul", dating the piece to the eighth century.

This fragment is constructed in the same style as the metal house-shaped book shrines known in Ireland around the same time. The stone measures twelve and a half inches long, seven inches wide and six inches high.

Many Anglo-Saxon rune memorials follow a similar layout in their wording and this example was a common commemorative formula. It seems that most of the rune-stones of this era were memorials or gravestones erected for wealthy patrons, as this memorial probably was.

THE KIRKHEATON STONE

carved by yew know who

This fragment of a larger runestone was discovered in the structure of the Kirkheaton Church in Kirkheaton village, Yorkshire. This piece of stone was reused as raw material by earlier masons in the rebuilding of the church. This same fate befell many other runestones which were only used for their practical value by the later stonemasons.

This fragment, difficult to date, records the Old English passage 'Eoh made this', and seems to have once belonged to a larger upright runestone memorial or otherwise of that period. Interestingly this runecarver's name is also cognate with *Eoh,* the rune representing the yew tree. The word 'Eoh' is also a common noun meaning horse or stallion, identical in meaning with other Anglo-Saxon names such as Hengist and Horsa, the legendary leaders of the first Anglo-Saxon settlers in Britian.

Displayed in the Tolson Memorial Museum in Huddersfield it is one of the few Anglo-Saxon runestones bearing the signature of the runecarver.

eoh   woro   htæ

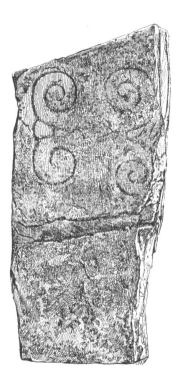

St Paul's Tombstone

black and white and red all over

Found in the last century this stone panel was once part of a sarcophagus situated in St. Paul's Churchyard in London where the stone was found.

An elegant beast traverses the stone with a snake entwined round its legs; this is a stylised reproduction of the lion and snake motif found on the Jelling Runestone in Jutland. It was originally painted in red, white and black with the runes following their archaic practice of being stained in red. The inscription details that, 'Ginna and Toki had this stone set up' in Scandinavian runes.

This stone is one of the most elegant and famous examples of the Ringerike style and was probably made during the reign of King Cnut (1016–35) who introduced it to England.

The stone is now in possession of the Museum of London where it can be seen.

23

THE KILBAR STONE
Vikings in the western isles

This rare Norse Christian gravestone was chanced upon in the old burial ground of the ruined church of Kilbarr on the remote island of Barra in the Outer Hebrides in 1865. It is displayed at the National Museum of Scotland, Edinburgh.

The stone is over six feet in length and through its runes is dated to the early eleventh century although their form on this inscription suggests the ninth century. This inscription is part of the first group of Norse runes to appear in Scotland, if not the oldest example. The front depicts a cross filled with flowing interlace formed from four bands. Decorative key patterns and S-scrolls are detailed outside.

The Old Norse inscription is set in two lines running vertically down the back of the stone and bears the following passage:

...ir	(th)kir(th)u	stinar	.....r	is	krus	sia	r..str
(ep)tir	(th)orgerdu	Steinar(s)	(dottu)r	es	kross	sja	reistr
'After	Thorgerth,	Steinar's	daughter,	this	cross	is	raised.'

24

THE ANDREAS III STONE
myths of heathen gods

The small but significant Isle of Man is home to over thirty Viking runic crosses, dated between the tenth and twelfth centuries and is the unique product of a Norse-Celtic society.

Kept in the Manx Museum in Douglas this cross fragment records the unfinished runic passage 'Thorvald erected this cross' using the Manx-Jeran Fuþark. Jeran is a district of Norway and is the probable origin of the Vikings who settled in Man.

Portrayed upon the stone are episodes from Heathen myths, the first detailing *Ragnarok*, the "Destiny of the Gods", in which Odinn, with a raven, thrusts a spear towards the mouth of the devouring Fenris wolf. Ragnarok may have been regarded as a religious metaphor for the ending of Heathenism. Odinn (OE *Woden*) according to legend was a master shaman and wizard and discovered the runes after hanging from Yggdrasil, the World Tree for nine nights. Through their discovery he became a god of speech, language and wisdom.

Counterbalanced on the other side of the stone is the god Thor (O.E. *Thunor*) holding his hammer and attempting to fish the world-serpent Jormungand from the sea.

Maeshowe no. 9

an Orkney lay

The Orkney islands nestle remotely on the shoulders of north-east Scotland, and close to the Loch of Harray on the mainland of Orkney is the impressive prehistoric mound known as Maeshowe. Within its chambers are contained the densest concentration of runic inscriptions found in any one place in the British Isles and are dated at around the eleven hundreds.

Situated on the north-west wall of the central chamber this amusing inscription's first two lines of runes translate into English thus: "Ingibjorg, the fair widow. Many a woman has gone stooping in here. A great show off."

The last line of characters are known as twig runes through their resemblance to twigs and were used to conceal a rune's identity. Left side strokes on the stave define the ættir (1-3) and the right side stroke would denote the hidden character in that ættir (1-8). Eg: the Proto-Germanic word *runa* in the Common Germanic Fuþark encodes as shown below. These twig runes utilise the ættir of the Orkney rune row and translate into the name Erlingr who probably carved the runes.

Maeshowe no. 20

carved with a magical axe

Built before 2700 BC the impressiveness of this ancient structure is reflected in the sunlight which shines directly down the entrance tunnel each winter solstice sunset and into the central chamber. The Maeshowe inscriptions are almost graffiti by comparison and were probably carved by sheltering Norsemen in the Tomb who used Scandinavian runes typical of the early Medieval period.

Situated on the chamber's south-east wall this inscription also utilises twig runes and records the passage "The man who is most skilled in runes west of the ocean carved these runes", but does not name this proud runemaster. The inscription is now connected to another in the chamber which mentions a legendary axe used to carve both.

Many of the other inscriptions, some in verse, tell of stolen treasure hidden elsewhere (noting the happiness of him who could find it), crusaders from Jerusalem who broke into the mound and a host of runemasters' names.

All the inscriptions of the Howe offer us a rare glimpse into the lives of these Viking adventurers who had settled on these tiny islands of the orcadians.

THE ROE-DEER BONE
some multiples of three

This tiny knuckle-bone, or astragalus, one inch in length, bears six runes incised across its surface and was found inside a cremation urn from the large Anglo-Saxon burial ground at Caistor-by-Norwich.

The runes, differently interpreted, probably translate as *raihan*, a likely personal-name, which has been identified as a likely cognate of Old English *raha*, 'roe-deer', denoting the actual creature which supplied the bone.

Also found inside this man's cremation urn were thirty-three bone counters, twenty-two white and eleven black, along with up to twenty-seven other assorted knuckle bones of roe-deer and sheep. Along with all of the astragali they may collectively represent an ancient symbolic game of some sort, or more likely the apparatus for casting lots, and all relate to the intriguing individual who was cremated. The number three was considered a highly magical number by the Anglo-Saxons, as were any of its multiples.

This unique artefact is accepted as bearing the oldest runic inscription in the country and is dated to the fifth century. It is on display at the Norwich Castle Museum.

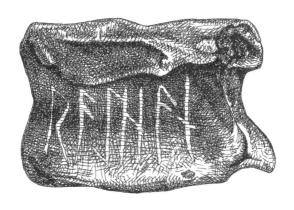

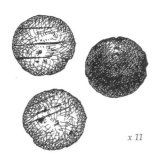

x 11

x 7

THE ALU FUNERARY URN

an intoxicating invocation

The prominent site at Spong Hill in Norfolk has been an occupation site since Mesolithic times and was used by the Anglo-Saxons as a burial ground. Archaeological excavations began in 1971, unearthing over 1700 cremation urns, mostly decorated, and digging still continues today.

This urn utilises a rune stamp around its curvature which is also used on other pots from the same site. Unusual in appearance, the runes resemble twig runes but are in fact double runes. Divided down their central axis they read out the common magical rune word *Alu* both forwards and backwards. *Alu* was used in conjunction with other magical words and appears in numerous European inscriptions between the third and the eighth centuries.

The word *Alu* has a basic meaning of 'ecstasy' or 'magic' and is cognate with the Old Norse word *Ol* and the Old English *Ealod*, or *Ealu*, both meaning 'ale', or 'beer'. Dated to the 5th century it can be seen at the Norwich Castle Museum.

THE RED-DEER ANTLER
from the strength of the stag

This inscription is found on the end protrusion of a Red Deer's antler along the tine, or sharp end, of the piece. Around five inches long it was found in the 1980s at the ancient Ango-Saxon settlement site in Brandon, Suffolk.

Fifteen Anglo-Saxon runes are inscribed, the last three worn down by wear and tear. Two words can readily be interpreted, *wohs*, cognate with OE *weox*, to grow or increase, and *wildum*, the ancestral cognate of the word 'wild'. The last five runes likely spell *deoran*, denoting a beast or animal.

Straightforward interpretation produces the statement 'grow wild animal' and leads to the literal truth that the piece grew on a wild animal. Interpreted symbolically the same statement suggests the owner may be utilising the magical power inherent in the animal, increasing the power of this amulet or knife-handle. The last rune is a *bindrune*, in this case a combination of the runes *Ac* and *Nyd*.

ᚹᚦᚻᛋᚹᛁᛚᛏᚻᚢᚻᚻᛗᚦᚱᛏ

w o h s w i l d u m d e o r a/n
w o h s   w i l d u m   d e o r a n

The Hunterston Brooch

a tenth century masterpiece

Dated to the early eighth century this attractive silver brooch was found in Hunterston, Ayrshire in Strathclyde. Five inches across it is one of the foremost examples of Celtic goldsmith art in the country. The front is decorated with pieces of amber

inlay and gilded sections of expert filigree gold work within which animals and snakes are detailed. The partly legible Scandinavian runes are dated to the tenth century with the first fifteen naming the Celtic owner and translating as "Melbrigda owns this brooch".

This finely crafted piece of expert workmanship can be seen at the national Museum of Scotland in Edinburgh.

THE FRANKS CASKET

and how a whale's life ended

The Franks Casket is displayed in the British Museum in London. This fascinating carved whalebone casket took its name from Sir Augustas W. Franks who acquired and donated most of its panels to the museum in 1867. Produced during the Dual Faith period the piece has been dated to the early eighth century through its use of the Anglian language. The casket measures nine inches long, seven and a half inches wide and five and a half inches high.

Anglo-Saxon runes spell out the name *ægili* on the top panel where a battle scene is also depicted. The name may refer to Egill, the brother of Welund, in an unrecorded scene from the myth, or to Aylesford, where Hengist and Horsa battled with King Vortigen and Horsa perished. The left scene on the front panel portrays an episode from the heathen myth of Welund. The right is an adoration of the Magi with the word 'Mægi' spelt in runes.

Around its perimeter the word 'whales bone' is recorded and also an alliterative verse detailing how through chasing fish onto shingle the whale's life ended.

41

The Franks Casket

continued

The back of the Casket (*below*) shows and tells Titus's capture of Jerusalem with his attacking spearmen. On the left panel (*opposite top*) is the classical scene of the she-wolf suckling Romulus and Remus. The heathen images on the right panel (*lower opposite*) may represent the ascension of a warrior into the afterlife, aided by the Wyrd sisters, the horse and the death bride.

The runes on the right panel total 72, twenty-four times a magical three. Particular runes on all panels are enlarged connecting their meaning with the imagery. The casket itself was devised as a portable magical system of protection for the owner, wishing him accumulation of wealth, victory in battle, protection at home, safe journeys and a heroic death.

THE AMULET RINGS

three survive

All bearing a similar magical inscription and dated from the eighth century this collection of talismanic rings were all found on the British mainland and mainly utilise the magical power of the number three and its multiples.

Found in Cumberland the top ring opposite is made of gold and depicts thirty runes, three of them on the inside band. The middle ring is made of electrum, an alloy of silver and gold; it bears thirty-three runes in three groups (*below*) and was found on Bramham Moor in Yorkshire. The bottom ring is made of pink agate, has thirty-two runes in eleven groups, and first appeared in an early Bristol collection.

The rune groups all follow the same rhyming pattern of Old English verse charms and contain certain unrecognisable word forms that the charms also implemented. Here the runes are used with rhyming sound magic possibly O.E Galderbrok, a spoken magical charm. The first and third ring are exhibited in the British Museum, whilst the second ring is held in the National Museum in Copenhagen.

ᚠᚱᚪᚱᛁᚢᚠᛚᛏ   ᚪᚱᛁᚢᚱᛁᚦᚩᚾ   ᚷᛚᚫᛋᛏᚫᛈᚫᚾᛏᚩᛚ

ærkriuflt   *kriurithon*   *glæstæpæn/tol*

ᛏᛅᛦᛅᚱᛁᚢᛅᚴᛏᛅᚱᛁᚢᚱᛁᚦᛁᛏᛜᚴᛐᛅᛏᚴᚴᛐ

ᛜᚠᛅᛦᛅᚱᛁᚢᚠᛐᛜᛅᚱᛁᚢᚱᛁᚦᛐᛜᚴᛐᛐᛐᚠᚴᚴᛐ

᛭᛬ᛗᛦᛅᚱᛁᚢᚠ᛫ᚢᛐᛐ᛫ᛅᚱᛁ᛫ᚢᚱᛁᚦᛐᚴᚴᛗᛌ᛫ᛐᛐ᛫ᚴᛐᛐᛗᛐᛐᛐ

45

The Thames Fitting

a magical cryptogram

This intricately detailed silver gilt dragon with blue glass eyes dates from the ninth century and was once the frontispiece of a gabled Shrine. Seven and a half inches long, it was found on the bed of the Thames in the last century and now belongs to the British Museum.

Translated into Old English the inscription defies straight-forward interpretation. The first seven runes are repeated in the

last eight characters of the inscription with the curious addition of the letter 'a'. This compares with similar rearrangements of ciphered words in Old English code texts. Letter groups are also formed when the runes are translated into the Roman alphabet, in use at the same time.

The unique grouping and layout of the characters indicate that the inscription probably represents a magical cryptogram. Remnants of the letter, word and sound magic that surrounded the runes are echoed here and probably precede the alphabet magic which flourished during the Middle Ages.

THE THAMES SCRAMASAX

an enchanted sword

An Anglo-Saxon short sword was known as a scramasax (OE *seaxor*) and this one was found in the bed of the Thames in 1857. Made of iron it measures over two feet in length.

This expensive weapon has its runes and ornamentation expertly inlaid with contrasting alloys of copper, bronze and silver and is dated to the late eighth century.

Twenty-eight characters of the Anglo-Saxon Fuþorc appear in sequence and demonstrate a singular development from the existing twenty-four rune Fuþark. This is the foremost

example found on the mainland where a complete Fuþorc of runes appear.

The maker or owner's name, Beagnoth, is inscribed across the single-sided blade and is a likely Kentish name, possibly indicating too a Kentish origin for the blade. The recording of whole rune rows was a common magical facilitator and protector in its own right, having the same use on this scramasax to protect or aide the owner. This rare artifact is in the possesion of the British Museum.

ᚠ ᚢ ᚦ ᚩ ᚱ ᚳ ᚷ ᚹ ᚻ ᚾ ᛁ ᛄ ᛇ ᛈ ᛉ ᛋ ᛏ ᛒ ᛖ ᛝ ᛞ ᛚ ᛗ ᛟ ᚪ ᚫ ᚣ ᛠ
f u þ o r c g w h n i j eo p x s t b e ŋ d l m œ a æ u ea

THE SUTTON SILVER DISC
another lost treasure

Found inside a lead casket along with about a hundred silver coins in 1634 when a plough turned it out of the soils of Cambridgeshire, this Anglo-Saxon brooch measures over six inches in diameter and has been dated to the early eleventh century. It is now in the British Museum, London.

Held between the nine pins on the front of the concave disc are four overlapping circles, each portraying a creature in zoomorphic design. Where the circles fuse a single eye motif is detailed. The back of the brooch contains an Old English Christian curse around its circumference against its theft.

The supporting plate across the back once detailed a complete inscription but is now broken and displays only a fragmentary text. The runes remain undeciphered because of their unique form but various suggestions have been made, that this is a poor reproduction by inexperienced hands or an intelligent attempt by a runemaster to develop cryptic runes.

A Symmetrical Hypothesis
nine twigs, nine worlds

> *"... for Woden took nine glory-twigs. He smote*
> *then the adder that it flew apart into nine parts."*

The angular shape of the runes primarily arose because the runes were a script designed to be inscribed upon staves of wood. The old English charm above, from the *Nine Herbs Charm* or *Lacnunga* (in Harley manuscript 585 in the British Museum) may mention a dual function of the runes. The first is that the nine glory twigs may have had runes etched upon them - a continuation of this oldest use. The second meaning lies in the fact that nine twigs can be arranged symmetrically to form a grid from which all runes can geometrically arise.

The hail rune, described by the rune poem as the frozen seed, bears an alternative six-fold shape in the Danish fuþark, echoing the symmetry of the grid, and led this rune to become modernly known as the 'mother rune'.

A Quantitive Puzzle

of fire and frost

Certain runes are repeated in other more complex rune-shapes, which display a symmetry of these simpler runes.

Breaking down the composition of these particular runes even further, the two most simple which can construct any one of them are *Kennaz* and *Isa*, the Elder *k* and *i* runes.

Heathen mythology records that the earth realm of the nine worlds were created out of the fusion of these polarities of fire and frost much like the eastern concept of yin and yang.

Perhaps together they quantitively fuse to produce the grid which defines and configures each succesive rune. These simple runeshapes are in fact the most common breakdown of every other rune and therefore may be the building blocks of all runeshapes.

	Name (Meaning)	Divinatory Meanings (Kennings)	Magical Correspondences	Deity Element Tree
ᚠ	*Feoh* (wealth)	survival, wealth, prosperity	*survival, well-being, resources*	*Frey, Freya, fire / earth, linden*
ᚢ	*Ur* (aurochs)	strength, healing, speed	*perseverance, healing, change*	*Urd, earth*
ᚦ	*Thorn* (thorn)	protection, emotional revelation	*passive protection, sudden illumination*	*Thunor, fire, Blackthorn, Oak*
ᚩ	*Os* (mouth)	communication, wisdom, learning	*wisdom, knowledge, communication*	*Woden, air, Ash*
ᚱ	*Rad* (riding)	journeys, advice, reception	*journeys, transferal, receiving*	*Thunor, air, Oak*
ᚳ	*Cen* (torch)	illumination, knowledge	*illumination, knowing, positivity*	*Freya, fire, Scots Pine*
ᚷ	*Gyfu* (gift)	gift, exchange, agreement	*balance, harmony, interchange*	*Gefjon, fire, Yew*
ᚹ	*Wynn* (joy)	happiness, joy, fulfilment	*wishing, fruition, well-being*	*Woden, air, Ash*
ᚻ	*Hægl* (hail)	disruption, cleansing	*transformation, regeneration*	*Hella, Urd, ice, Yew*
ᚾ	*Nyd* (need)	necessities, duty, friction	*needs, binding, hopes*	*Loki, Sculd, ice, Ivy*
ᛁ	*Is* (ice)	clarity, stillness, impediment	*clarity, lucidity, stopping flow*	*Verdandi, ice Yew*
ᛄ	*Ger* (harvest)	harvest, returns	*completion, fruition*	*Frigg, earth Apple*
ᛇ	*Eoh* (yew)	defence, action, purpose	*protection, defence, warding*	*Uller, ice, Yew*
ᛈ	*Peor þ* (birth)	birth, revelation, rediscovery	*revelation, initiation*	*Frigg, water, Birch*
ᛉ	*Eolhx* (elk-sedge)	protection, warding, creativity	*channelling, protection, stability*	*Heimdall, air Oak*
ᛋ	*Sigel* (sun)	light, health, well-being	*sudden illumination, healing*	*Baldæg, Sunna fire, Oak*

56

	NAME (MEANING)	DIVINATORY MEANINGS (KENNINGS)	MAGICAL CORRESPONDENCES	DEITY ELEMENT TREE
↑	*Tir* (Tiw)	legalities, battles, competitiveness	*victory, justice, directness*	*Tiw,* fire, Ash
ᛒ	*Beorc* (birch)	motherhood, maturity, provision	*purification, nurturing, completion*	*Frigg,* water, earth, Birch
ᛗ	*Eh* (horse)	partnership, loyalty, journeys	*movements, journeys, trust*	*Hengest/Horsa,* water, Linden
ᛘ	*Man* (mankind)	humanity, friendship	*cooperation, reason, respect*	*Heimdall,* water, Holly
ᚱ	*Lagu* (water)	emotions, womanhood	*intuition, fertility, psychic powers*	*Njord,* water, Willow
ᛝ	*Ing* (Ing)	growth, change, transition	*new beginnings, plenty*	*Ing,* earth, Apple
ᛟ	*Eþel* (home)	property, family, home	*inheritance, ancestry*	*Woden,* earth, Ash
ᛞ	*Dæg* (day)	change, balance, positivity	*light, balance, openings*	*Esotara,* fire, Oak
ᚪ	*Ac* (oak)	growth, faith, patience	*potential, increase*	*Thunor,* fire, Oak
ᚫ	*Aesc* (ash)	communication, information	*intellect, expression*	*Woden,* Air Ash
ᛖ	*Yr* (axe-ham)	defence, action, protection	*defence, finding*	*Ullr,* ice Yew
ᛡ	*Iar* (river fish)	stability, accord, contentment	*harmony, lucky star*	*Iar,* water Willow
ᛠ	*Ear* (grave)	conclusions, returnings, endings	*endings, completion, renewal*	*Erce,* earth, Yew

As a magical script the runes were used to foretell what was to come and also to effect change. The earliest account of runic divination is recorded by the Roman historian and traveller Tacitus in his Germania. Symbols, probably runes, were etched upon staves of wood taken from a fruit-bearing tree, scattered, and then three staves were taken and read by the officiant. Perhaps known in the Old English vocabulary as a runwita or rune-knower, they acted as counsellors and advisors and would have been runcræftig, rune-skilled. This old threefold method of divination is today known as asking the Norns, or the three sisters of Wyrd (OE), fate or destiny, representing the past, present and future. The runes are believed to invoke this power of wyrd both to read the future and for personal guidance and transformation. The runes also relate intimately to the Heathen Deities that name each day of our week. Mythologically they are primarily connected with Woden, their legendary discoverer after whom Wednesday is named.

NOTES